CHARLES RICHARD DREW, M.D.

CHARLES RICHARD DREW, M.D.

RINNA EVELYN WOLFE

A First Book
Franklin Watts   1991
New York   London   Toronto   Sydney

The author wishes to thank several people who encouraged the writing of this book: my friends Anne Fox, Frances Whitney, and Glenna Goulet; Esmy Bhan and Dr. Doris Hull at the Moorland-Spingarn Archives of Howard University; Joe and Grace Drew, who offered advice and kind hospitality; and my editor, Mary Perrotta.

Cover photograph courtesy of Historical Pictures Service, Chicago.

All photographs courtesy of Moorland-Spingarn Research Center, Howard University except: American Red Cross: pp. 30, 38 bottom, 43, 44, 58.

Library of Congress Cataloging-in-Publication Data

Wolfe, Rinna.
Charles Richard Drew, M.D. / by Rinna Evelyn Wolfe
p.   cm. — (A First book.)
Includes bibliographical references (p.   ) and index.
Summary: A biography of the noted physician, focusing on his discovery of methods for separating plasma from blood.
ISBN 0-531-20021-3
1. Drew, Charles Richard, 1904–1950—Juvenile literature. 2. Surgeons—United States—Biography—Juvenile literature. 3. Afro-American surgeons—United States—Biography—Juvenile literature. 4. Blood—Collection and preservation—History—Juvenile literature.
[1. Drew, Charles Richard, 1904–1950. 2. Physicians. 3. Afro-Americans—Biography. 4. Blood.] I. Title. II. Series.
RD27.35.D74W65   1991
617'.092—dc20
[B]
[92]   90-13106 CIP AC

CONTENTS

INTRODUCTION

Snow flurries fell on the shivering stadium crowd. Football fans held their breath, waiting for the final play between Amherst College and Wesleyan Institute. The teams were battling for the 1923 championship, and Amherst trailed 6–10.

Amherst called signals. The Wesleyan defense rushed in, climbing all over Charlie Drew, the black sophomore halfback. Dragging his tacklers along, Charlie sent the pigskin flying downfield 40 yards. Quarterback John McBride caught the ball in midair for an amazing touchdown. Victory!

Charlie became an instant campus hero. Over the next two years he led his team to its largest scores in history. Looking back years later, Coach

Tuss McLaughry said, "He could have played on any team in the country. . . . Charlie Drew was the best player I ever coached."

But a sports career did not attract Charlie. He decided to be a doctor, and the scientific ideas he pioneered helped save millions of lives.

CHAPTER
1
EARLY YEARS

Charles Richard Drew was born on June 3, 1904, in his grandmother's house in Washington, D.C. His father, Richard Thomas Drew, a carpet layer, was the only black in the Carpet and Tile Layers Union. His mother, Nora Burrell Drew, a graduate of Howard University's Miner Normal School in Washington, D.C., was a homemaker.

The Drews lived near the White House in a locale called Foggy Bottom, so named because of dense mists from the Potomac River. A mix of Irish, Italian, French, and black people lived in their neighborhood.

Richard and Nora, devoted parents, encouraged their children to aim high, and to do what they believed in. They taught Charlie and the younger children, Elsie, Joseph, Nora, and Eva,

Charlie and his siblings were encouraged to take their studies very seriously. Pictured here are Charlie (tallest boy), Joseph, Nora, and Elsie.

to be responsible—to set the table, wash dishes, clean house, and care for their clothes. Charlie later joked that surgical training came easy because he had learned to sew as a child.

The Drew children used their capital city well. They rolled Easter eggs on the White House lawn, enjoyed picnics and free concerts at the Washington Monument, and often visited the museums and public buildings.

Charlie grew up in a comfortable home filled with books and classical music. On Sundays the family prayed and read the Bible together. Then they attended the Nineteenth Street Baptist Church, where Richard sang and taught the junior choir. Evenings, with Richard accompanying on guitar or piano, friends often joined the Drews in spirited family songfests.

Charlie was a natural athlete. Although Washington, D.C., public swimming pools were *segregated* (black and white people had to use separate facilities), Richard Drew taught his sons to swim at a local pool open to blacks. Before long, Charlie and Joe were splashing and diving in the Potomac River. When he was eight, Charlie won four medals at a Fourth of July swim meet. That was only the beginning.

A hard worker, Richard Drew earned enough

for everyday needs, but there was no money for extras. So when Charlie was twelve and wanted spending money, he became a newspaper boy for the *Washington Times* and the *Evening Star.* With his brother Joe's help, he increased his routes and hired six boys to work for them. Often they sold 2,000 papers a day. Two years later, Charlie became a special-delivery boy for the United States Post Office, and nine-year-old Joe inherited the newspaper business.

Charlie graduated from Stevens Elementary School and entered Paul Laurence Dunbar High, which was the best black college-preparatory school in the country. Named in honor of the black poet, it had a staff of teachers, scholars themselves, who inspired their students to excellence.

Charlie quickly became a four-letter man—a star in football, basketball, baseball, and track. He captained a high school cadet corps and twice received the James E. Walker medal as the school's best all-around athlete.

In the early 1900s the world did not have the medicines we have today. After World War I a global epidemic of influenza took 20 million lives. Charlie read that this number included 500,000

A talented athlete, Charlie was a star football and basketball player. He is standing fourth from the right with Dunbar's basketball team (top) and third from the right with the football team (bottom).

Americans. Two years later he watched his sister Elsie die of another disease, tuberculosis. Though only fifteen, for the first time he imagined himself becoming a doctor.

Sad and in mourning for Elsie, the family decided to leave the unhealthy weather of Foggy Bottom. They moved across the river to the healthier climate of Arlington, Virginia, where they lived in a two-story house.

During high school vacations, Charlie worked on construction sites. The outdoor labor kept him physically fit. One year a teacher sent a dozen Dunbar students to work in a glass factory in Salem, New Jersey.

Charlie had never been so far from home. He was well paid, but the hauling and shoveling of sand near a furnace heated well over 100°F (37.8°C) was strenuous work. One by one boys left, but not Charlie. Not one to quit, he stayed until summer's end.

Sometimes Charlie neglected his schoolwork, but not for long. His parents insisted that he study harder and he did, especially his favorite subjects, biology and math. His effort paid off because at graduation in 1922 he was awarded a partial scholarship to Amherst College in Massachusetts.

CHAPTER
2
A TROUBLED STAR AT AMHERST

At Amherst Charles moved into an almost all-white world. Solidly built, he was a handsome six-footer, with brown hair touched with red. He attracted much attention with his sparkling brown eyes and courteous manners. He was usually soft-spoken, but when angered, his light-skinned face flushed deep pink. Before long his classmates nicknamed him Big Red.

On campus Charles reunited with Dunbar buddies Monty Cobb, Bill Hastie, and Mercer Cook. He joined Omega Psi Phi, the second-oldest black fraternity in the country, and with Mercer Cook he wrote the fraternity's national hymn. Sometimes he strummed on a ukelele a tune of his own that his frat brothers called "Charlie's Blues."

Charles liked the Amherst liberal-arts curriculum, but from the beginning, he focused more on sports than on academics. Incredibly fast, and breaking records as a sprinter and hurdle-jumper, he became the only freshman to win a major letter. And his agility with a football made him not only a celebrity but also a target on the football field.

Once a tackler left a metal cleat from his shoe in Charles's thigh, and Charles landed in the hospital. He now knew how it felt to be "banged up." Thinking it was time to learn more about how the body works, he became a keen student of anatomy.

Normally, Amherst students elected a man with Charles's ability to be captain of the football team. But two other talented black athletes had already been passed over. Now, so was Charles. After student protests, he was voted

Charles continued to earn athletic glory at Amherst College. Scientific history would have been very different had he decided to pursue sports rather than medicine as a career.

captain of the track team, and the Thomas W. Ashley trophy acknowledged him as Amherst's most valuable player.

Yet, despite the honors, Charles never forgot one experience with the track team. After a competition with Brown University, the Amherst team planned to have dinner at the Narragansett Hotel, but the hotel manager would not serve "colored boys." *Colored* and *Negro* were the usual terms people used when they talked about black people before the 1960s. The track coach suggested that the four black team members dine on Brown's campus instead. The ride home that night was long and silent.

In college, Charles was at best an average student. He once made a perfect score on an important chemistry exam, and he earned straight A's in biology. Mostly, however, his grades ranged from A's to D's. He won no academic honors, but received the Howard Hill Mossman trophy for

Although he did study hard in subjects he enjoyed, Charles's most memorable achievements at Amherst were sports oriented.

bringing the most athletic glory to Amherst. More important, when he graduated he decided to study medicine.

But there were problems. Even with his scholarship and part-time jobs, Charles had accumulated debts. Medical school would have to wait until he paid bills and saved enough to pay his way. Thus, for the next two years, he taught biology and chemistry and coached at Morgan College, a small black college in Baltimore, Maryland.

A beloved teacher, Charles Drew always coaxed his students to excel. He turned a raggedy football team and second-rate basketball team into champions. Then he prepared to move on.

To his surprise, Howard University rejected his application to medical school because he lacked two credits in English. Instead they offered him a job as assistant football coach.

Angry and hurt—they had not even suggested that he make up the work—Charles declined the job. He wrote that if his English was not good enough for medical school, he doubted that he was good enough to join their staff.

But he told his brother Joe, "Someday I'll come back and run this place."

CHAPTER
3
NORTH TO CANADA

Howard University's rejection proved to be a blessing. Weeks later McGill University in Montreal, Canada, which unlike other schools did not ask what race Charles belonged to, accepted him into their five-year medical program.

To Charles, Canadians seemed color-blind. He could go anywhere and he could eat wherever he wished. He enjoyed being accepted for who he was. He plunged eagerly into his studies.

Charles excelled at McGill. Soon he was elected into Alpha Phi Omega, the honor society for medical students. Despite the heavy workload, he also made time for sports.

Canadians encouraged their graduate students to enter intercollegiate events. So Charles once again competed and won championships for high and low hurdles and broad jumps. Years later, when a crowd found out he was a spectator at their football game, they burst into wild cheers. Charles remained an athletic hero all his life.

At McGill, Charles lived modestly. He received a small sum from his father, and he waited on tables. Sometimes Joe sent money, but Charles never had enough.

On New Year's Eve 1929, he wondered what 1930 would bring. All alone, he wrote gloomily, ". . . ten cents for tea and toast. I was cold from walking all over the city. . . ." He longed to mingle with the laughing couples he had passed. To console himself, he wrote on: "Today I haven't been hungry. I was well dressed. I am not sick . . . I have a dollar. I couldn't go very far on a dollar, not even alone . . . I am afraid to spend it . . . tomorrow I must eat . . . and many days after that. . . . Tomorrow I have been invited to dinner, but the next day?"

Charles never let friends pay for him. When he told them he was broke they thought he had overspent his allowance. No one knew he lived for a whole week on the ten dollars his father sent, or that his family did without so that he could continue at school.

Charles's brother, left, and father, center,
both tried to ease Charles's financial burden
while he studied at McGill.

Once Charles wrote Tuss McLaughry, his Amherst coach, that he might have to quit waiting on tables since an old football injury was acting up. Knowing Charles would never accept charity, McLaughry collected hundreds of dollars from former Amherst classmates. Then he sent the money as a loan. When Charles became Dr. Drew, he gratefully repaid every dollar. That fall Charles won a Rosenwald scholarship, a prestigious award for the education of black students. The money made him feel secure, at least temporarily.

Charles impressed his professors, especially Dr. John Beattie, his anatomy instructor. A visitor from England and only five years older than his student, Beattie was doing blood research that fascinated Charles. Before long, Charles was reading everything he could find on blood: the early discoveries, blood's composition, the scientists who explored it, experiments of the past, and the history and use of transfusions. Sharing common interests in sports and blood research, Charles and Beattie became friends and began to do experiments together.

Charles visited Montreal General Hospital frequently to watch Beattie test for blood types. Before Karl Landsteiner, an Austrian doctor, discovered blood types in 1901, and before doctors knew that a patient's and a donor's blood had to match, patients often died from transfusions.

Now doctors recognized four main blood types: A, B, AB, and O. A type-O person may supply blood to all groups, and an AB person may receive blood from all types.

One day when a patient needed a transfusion and his sister's blood did not match, Charles volunteered his own. This was not a first. He and other resident doctors routinely donated when blood was needed. But he worried.

Hospitals, he thought, should not have to call for fresh blood. They should be able to keep stored blood on hand for emergencies. Beattie shared his concern and urged him to investigate further.

In 1933, Charles graduated with the degrees of doctor of medicine and master of surgery. He also won the Williams Prize, given to the best senior in the class. He then interned at the Montreal General and Royal Victoria hospitals, where he polished his surgical skills and continued to research the preservation of blood.

Toward the end of his residency, he applied to teach pathology at Freedmen's Hospital in Washington, D.C. Its clinic was connected to

This experimental blood bank vault was
developed from a necessity for doctors
and hospitals to store blood so that it would
always be available when a patient needed it.

Howard Medical School. This time Howard accepted him willingly. His starting salary was $150
a month, slightly more than he had earned as a
paperboy. Dr. Charles Richard Drew headed south
from Canada, back home.

CHAPTER
4
WASHINGTON, D.C., AND NEW YORK

Drew returned to Washington, D.C., in 1937, just before America emerged from the Great Depression. Across the sea, the German dictator Adolf Hitler was arming his country for war. At Howard University, Dean Numa P.G. Adams was making major changes. He and Dr. Edward Lee Howes, who directed Howard's medical school, wanted dedicated men like Drew on their staff. Dr. Howes would later say, "Drew . . . taught well, showed good judgment, and had practically no race prejudice."

Howard University was established in 1867 for black students. Freedmen's Hospital was called the "Jim Crow" shack. "Jim Crow" was an expression referring to any law or practice used to segregate blacks. Badly equipped and poorly staffed, the hospital had been founded five years before the university. Its patients, mostly black, came from both nearby and faraway states because they were not admitted to white hospitals for treatment.

Only five or six medical schools accepted black students. And after graduation, finding a residency in a United States hospital was even more difficult for them. So Drew resolved to educate the surgeons at Freedmen's to be the best that could be found anywhere.

In the mid 1930s, a second world war loomed in Europe. Dr. Drew realized blood would be crucial for treating the wounded. So, along with all his responsibilities, he continued to research the storage of blood.

In 1938, Drew received a two-year Rockefeller Foundation fellowship and took a leave from Howard. He immediately left for New York City, where he took advanced training in pre- and post-operative care at Columbia University and Presbyterian Hospital.

Studying with Dr. John Scudder, he worked on the chemistry of blood and its use in transfusions. His vast knowledge about blood experiments done in the Soviet Union and at Cook County Hospital in Chicago became invaluable to Scudder's project.

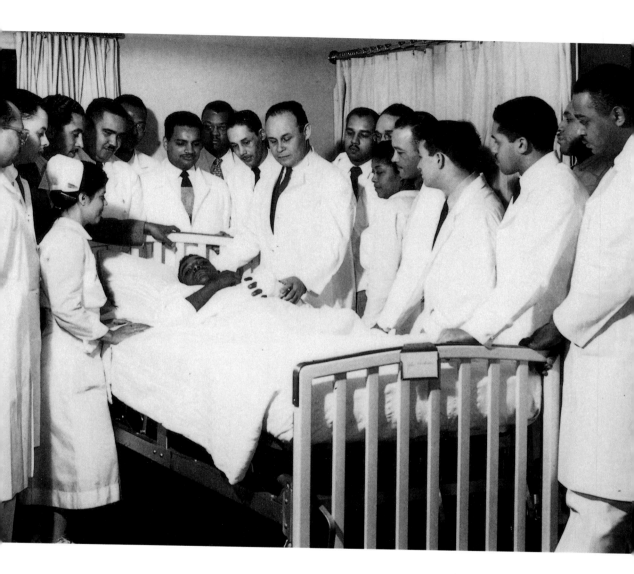

Dr. Drew, center, teaches students
at Freedmen's Hospital. He was
determined to give them the best
education he could.

Dr. Drew worked with patients, but also
experimented in the laboratory to find out
everything there was to know about
blood and its components.

At this time most blood was transfused from one live body to another. Whole blood spoiled quickly even when refrigerated. Scudder and Drew agreed that they must find a safe way to preserve blood.

Charles Drew was used to working long hours. His days began early and ended near midnight. After mornings in surgery, he joined biologists, chemists, pathologists, and technicians in a well-equipped laboratory where they conducted hundreds of experiments. They tested day-old, week-old, and older blood to observe cell changes. They kept accurate records about the chemicals that prevented blood from clotting and what caused red cells to weaken. And Drew designed a flask that separated red cells from plasma.

He began to study plasma, the yellowish liquid in blood, because it contained hundreds of elements necessary to life. One was *fibrinogen*, a protein that causes blood to clot. Drew realized that since plasma itself does not contain red cells, it did not have a blood type. Thus it could be given to everyone. Perhaps, he thought, plasma would help solve the storage problem, but how?

Mid-year, Drew decided to work toward a doctorate of science. No black doctor had ever earned this degree. He knew he was making history. He also knew he was making it easier for those black physicians coming after him.

His original research led to an invitation to speak at Tuskegee Institute in Alabama. The trip changed his life.

On the way to the conference, he stopped off in Atlanta, Georgia, to visit his college buddy Mercer Cook. At a candlelit dinner, Mercer introduced him to Minnie Lenore Robbins, a willowy, pretty teacher who taught home economics at Spelman College. Nearly thirty-five years old, Charles Drew promptly fell in love. Years later Lenore said, "The moment I saw him I knew he was a man to be reckoned with."

Returning north from Alabama three nights later, Drew stopped again in Atlanta. Hiring a cab, he hurried to Lenore's dormitory and knocked loudly on her door until she woke up. In the chilly night he proposed. Then he spent the next six months courting her with love letters filled with his dreams and plans. When Marian Anderson sang before 75,000 people at the steps of the Lincoln Memorial because the Daughters of the American Revolution refused to let her sing in Constitution Hall, Drew wrote:

In all my life I have never seen such an impressive thing. With the soft rays of pink

When Lenore met Charles, she knew
that he was no ordinary suitor.

3 A.M. 4/13/39

Dear Lenore, Just in from giving another
talk before the Manhattan Medical
Society, but I must get a word off
to you before turning in.

Seems ages since I left
you standing in the window as we
pulled out—a lovely picture that
completely filled my vision as the
miles sped by. Lowell left me to
my thoughts and we came to Charlotte
in the evening with hardly a word
having been passed. We spent
Friday night with an old friend
of his, Dr. Green and left early
Saturday morning for Oxford. 16.

Drew's letters were not only
eloquent, but were also beautiful to
look at—his handwriting was exquisite!

sun gleaming against the white marble beauty . . . she raised her exquisite voice in song and lifted with a sweep of melody a whole race to higher levels of thoughts, feeling and hope. Countless thousands paid her the tribute of almost reverent silence when she sang. . . . She held them beneath her magic sway, making them laugh or sigh . . . and when she finished with "Nobody knows de trouble I've seen," many eyes were moist with unashamed tears and hearts too full for words.

On September 23, 1939, the couple married and moved into a modest apartment near Drew's laboratory. At the time of his marriage, Drew owned two well-worn suits and shoes with cracks. He earned less than $100 a month, but somehow the happy couple managed.

Lenore soon realized that a doctor's life was not glamorous. Wanting to see her busy husband regularly, she joined his staff. Early on she accepted the fact that medicine would be her lifelong rival for Charles's affection.

CHAPTER
5
WORLD WAR II AND BLOOD BANKS

Just before Charles and Lenore married, New York's Presbyterian Hospital started a blood bank program. Dr. Scudder became director of the laboratory. Dr. Drew supervised the clinical testing.

He carried a workload that would tire most people. But whenever Lenore asked him to slow down, he said, "I'm a sprinter, remember?" He did tough jobs with grace.

Besides performing surgery and researching blood, Drew had begun to write his required doctoral thesis. He called his paper "Banked Blood: A Study in Blood Preservation." The 245-page document traced the history of blood and told how preserved blood changes. It also described his original experiments and how he organized an efficient blood-bank program. Though it was never published, it became the prime guide for the country's future blood banks.

In 1939, German troops marched into several European countries. Then in June 1940, Germany began a ferocious attack on France. Fighting for its life, France needed a huge supply of blood for its wounded. Soon Scudder and Drew were invited to an emergency meeting called by the Blood Transfusion Association. Nobel prize winner Karl Landsteiner (the discoverer of blood types), Max Stumia (the inventor of a machine to dry plasma), Army officials, and Dr. Alexis Carrel, a Nobel Prize-winning French surgeon, were in the room.

After Dr. Carrel appealed for help for his country, Drew explained his plasma work. The men debated for hours and finally agreed. Although America was officially neutral, it would begin a "Plasma for France" project. But before a single shipment could be made, German soldiers cut through the Maginot line of defense and occupied French soil. With the fall of France, the program stalled.

In June 1940, Drew received his doctor of science in surgery from Columbia University. After-

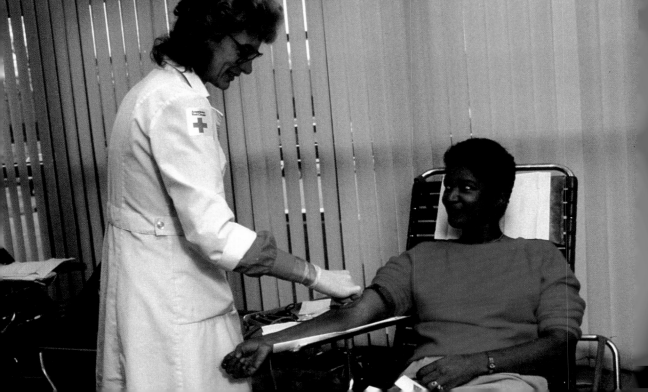

ward he wrote to a friend that the new degree felt "like the day after a big race is won . . . only in medicine it takes much longer."

Exactly a year after Presbyterian Hospital's blood bank opened, Lenore gave birth to their first child, "Bebe" Roberta. Her nickname stood for *blood bank.*

Dr. Drew could have opened a private practice and eventually become rich. Instead, he returned south with two promotions: instructor of surgery at Howard University and assistant surgeon at Freedmen's Hospital. He was ready to prove that black doctors could be more than small-town practitioners. But events of history shortened his stay.

In the fall, German bombs blitzed Great Britain night and day. Cities crumbled. Thousands died, and thousands more were wounded. On September 1, 1940, Drew received a cable

This staff of an early blood bank
(top) saved lives by collecting and
banking blood for use at a later date.
Dr. Drew is seated in the center.
Today, many people donate blood regularly
through the American Red Cross.

from John Beattie, his teacher-friend from Mc-Gill. Now a director at England's Royal College of Surgeons, Beattie asked:

COULD YOU SECURE FIVE THOUSAND AMPULES DRIED PLASMA FOR TRANS-FUSION WORK IMMEDIATELY AND FOLLOW THIS BY EQUAL QUANTITY IN THREE OR FOUR WEEKS.

Drew did not believe that that much plasma existed in the world. But he knew he would not let his friend down.

Howard University granted Dr. Drew a second leave. Within weeks he returned to New York City as medical supervisor of the "Blood for Britain" program.

He brought blood donors together at one location, recruiting them through radio announcements, billboards, newspapers, and subway posters. During the first five months of the program, 14,566 people showed up to give blood. After Drew's small, well-trained staff tested and sterilized the blood at Columbia's Presbyterian Hospital, it was sent to England.

When the British began to fill their own needs, Drew's program ended; he now shifted his con-

Here, blood is being readied for
shipment to Great Britain in the
"Blood for Britain" drive.

cern to finding a way to mass-produce plasma. He and his staff solved the problem by *drying* plasma. It could then be turned back into liquid plasma by mixing it with water. Dried plasma could now be shipped in safe packages to wherever it was needed.

In February 1941, the United States Armed Forces asked the Red Cross to organize American blood banks. Dr. Drew was appointed assistant director of this national program. He immediately established the highest standards as he trained many staffs and volunteers. Using mobile units, he directed the openings of blood collection centers nationwide. When Japan bombed Pearl Harbor on December 7, 1941, the United States had an ample supply of plasma on hand.

Segregation had always been an accepted way of life in the armed services. Blacks, kept in separate regiments, received less training than white soldiers and usually did the menial jobs. Few were ever promoted to the rank of officer. Armed services units were not desegregated until 1951.

Unfortunately, in 1941, the U.S. War Department created a policy of blood segregation, which the American Red Cross accepted. The Army ordered the collection of Caucasian blood only.

Dr. Charles Drew (left) is pictured here with doctors, nurses, and drivers from a mobile unit of New York Presbyterian Hospital. This was the first mobile unit to collect blood plasma for the "Blood for Britain" program.

Black soldiers did, however, sometimes give blood for each other within black units.

Drew asked that the order be canceled, but his request was not honored. Respected as he was for his work with plasma, even he did not qualify as a donor. Feeling that this rule insulted his people, he called a press conference. Speaking as a scientist, he told reporters, "The blood of individual human beings may differ by grouping, but there is absolutely no scientific basis for any difference according to race."

In April 1941, Drew resigned from his post with the Red Cross. That same month he received his surgeon's certificate from the American Board of Surgery. Months later he would become the first black surgeon to serve on that board. Some people believed he had left the Red Cross because of the Army's blood segregation policy. But his wife later said, "I'd never known Charlie to run from a fight."

In 1941, Dr. Charles Drew
returned to Howard—the college
that had rejected his medical
school application—to become the
head of the department of surgery.

Drew returned to Howard because he had promised to, and because he became head of the department of surgery. Besides, years earlier he had predicted he would be back "to run the place."

Months after Pearl Harbor was attacked, he learned that plasma had helped save the lives of thousands of servicemen and civilians. Dr. Charles Drew had done his job well.

CHAPTER
6
HOME TO STAY

Drew returned to Howard determined that his graduate doctors would be as good as doctors anywhere. He was a tough taskmaster with strict rules. He himself did not smoke, drink, curse, or gamble. And he expected almost perfect behavior from his students and staff alike.

Once when he saw a young student dressed sloppily, Drew told him, "Well, *I'll* wash your clothes. *I'll* darn your socks." The embarrassed man never dressed that way again.

Drew was as generous as he was firm. He tutored those in need of help, and sometimes paid out of his own pocket for student trips to important medical meetings. While his students watched him operate, he explained why he used

Drew was more than a teacher, he was
personally involved with his
students and cared about them.

the instruments he did. And he encouraged the most talented to apply to better-equipped, mainly white institutions for additional training.

The day his first graduate students took their exams before the American Board of Surgery he fretted nervously. To stay calm, he hammered an old coal bin to pieces in his basement. Later, after receiving word that "his boys" had placed first and second on the exam, he grinned like a proud papa.

A loving man, Charles kept in touch with his students after they graduated. Most of them went on to excel in different specialized fields of surgery.

Dr. Drew began to receive many awards— from Tuskegee, the E. S. Jones award (1943), an honorary degree from Virginia State (1945), and the National Association for the Advancement of Colored People (NAACP) Spingarn Medal in 1944. This prestigious medal is given to a black American who contributes the most to humankind. In 1944 Drew also became chief-of-staff at Freedmen's Hospital.

He joined the American-Soviet Committee on Science (1943) and became a fellow of the International Surgeons (1946). He also served on many boards, among them, the National Society of

Crippled Children and a local chapter of the American Cancer Society. But Dr. Drew never became a member of the American Medical Association (AMA) because the Washington, D.C., chapter was segregated.

The national AMA was founded in 1847 to improve the quality of health care around the nation. Officially its rules did not deny membership because of race, creed, or color. But each local group could choose its own members. Though black doctors did publish in the AMA journal (Drew himself contributed twenty-one articles), few blacks were invited into chapters.

Not being AMA members meant black doctors could not treat their patients at local white hospitals. Arguing against this discrimination, in 1947 Drew wrote to Dr. Morris Fishbein (editor of the AMA journal):

The men in . . . the nation's capital are still rejected although there can be no doubt about their qualifications. . . . In Freedmen's Hospital . . . a man must successfully pass his speciality board. . . . The chief of every department is a certified specialist. . . . Match these standards with those of the great hospitals of the land and they will

This is the Eagles Nest that Hitler built on one of the highest peaks in the Bavarian Alps. From here he hoped to look over a conquered world. He built too high. Daddy

7-12-49

Charles R. Drew Jr.

328 College St. N.V

Washington, D.C

U.S.A,

This postcard to Charles Jr.,
mailed in 1949, revealed Charles
Sr.'s thoughts on Hitler.

be found good; but the AMA will not grant them the privilege of discussing common problems with fellow physicians. . . . One hundred years of racial bigotry . . . one hundred years with no progress report. A sorry record.

Drew asked for the rule to be changed, but this did not happen in his lifetime.

In 1949, four years after World War II ended, he served as a consultant to the Army surgeon-general and toured U.S. hospitals in Occupied Europe. This trip was his first holiday.

He wrote home about "shabby hospitals, 15–20 years behind U.S. centers," and described postwar cities "with buildings standing stark against the sky with empty windows like the hollow eyes of skeletons." He raved about the music he heard in Vienna, "all kinds from Beethoven to very good swing." He asked Lenore to save his letters and postcards for their children.

After a quick tour of Paris he wrote her, "Someday we must see this place together." But that trip was not to be.

CHAPTER
7
THE AUTO ACCIDENT

Charles Drew sprinted through life working as though he alone must change the world. Although he didn't spend as much time at home as he wanted, he was devoted to his children. Off duty, he relaxed by cooking, gardening, playing the piano, or going to Western movies.

As chief-of-staff, he frequently represented his hospital at conferences. On March 31, 1950, after performing several operations, Drew attended a Howard University student council banquet. Then he napped briefly before joining three other doctors for a long, early-morning drive to Tuskegee, Alabama.

He was tired, but after a coffee stop he took his turn at the wheel. He dozed for a moment, and in that instant the car swerved off the road. He woke and tried to steer. It was too late. At 8 A.M. on April 1, on Route 49 outside Burlington, North Carolina, the car flipped over three times.

Everyone escaped with minor injuries except Drew. With a crushed chest and a leg cut to the bone, he was barely breathing.

Drew was rushed by ambulance to the Alamance General Hospital near Burlington. There, three white doctors tried to save him, but his damaged chest blocked the blood flow to his heart. He died two hours later. He was forty-five years old.

Thousands mourned his death. Besides his widow, Drew left four children: Bebe Roberta, aged nine, Charlene Rosella, eight, Rhea Sylvia, six, and Charles Richard, Jr., four. Also surviving him were his mother, Nora, aged seventy, his brother, Joe, and sisters, Nora and Eva.

Unfortunately, the Drew
children would have to
grow up without their father.
His achievements, however,
would survive as his legacy.

Charles Drew was a generous man who would help anyone. Yet he never earned a large salary. A tax return shows his 1947 income as $8,199. What he gave the world, however, cannot be measured by money.

Today, schools, hospitals, clinics, and library rooms across the country bear his name. His portrait hangs in the American Red Cross building and the National Portrait Gallery in Washington, D.C., and at the National Institute of Health in Bethesda, Maryland.

On June 3, 1981, the seventy-seventh year of his birth, the U.S. Postal Service issued a thirty-five-cent stamp honoring Dr. Drew in the Great American Series. And in 1986 a six-foot marker was placed on the site of the fateful accident.

Thirty-nine years after his death, 1,200 citizens honored him at a black-tie dinner in the nation's capital. On October 12, 1989, Howard University presented the first Charles Richard Drew World Medicine Prizes to two black doctors.

This image appears on
the postal stamp honoring
Dr. Drew.

Dr. Harold Amos, aged seventy, of Harvard Medical School, and Benjamin Osuntokun, aged fifty-four, chief medical director of a hospital in Ibadan, Nigeria, received $50,000 each for their lifelong efforts to improve universal health.

Dr. Amos has given his award to a Harvard scholarship fund for minority students. Dr. Osuntokun will start small medical stations in his country. Both men carry on the ideals Charles Richard Drew lived. Justice for everyone and service for others were what Dr. Drew believed life is all about.

This portrait shows
Dr. Charles Richard Drew
experimenting—the way
he would always be
remembered by the
scientific community.

GLOSSARY

Ampule—a small sealed glass container used to hold a solution for injection.

Anatomy—the structure of an organism or any of its parts.

Bigotry—behavior showing the prejudice of a person who is not tolerant of other people's race, opinions, and beliefs.

Caucasian—related to the white race, as classified by physical features.

Cleat—a spike-like piece on the bottom of a shoe that allows for a better grip on the ground; commonly found on sports shoes.

Clotting—a process by which fluid blood hardens into a thickened mass.

Epidemic—outbreak of a disease that affects many people at once.

Fibrinogen—a protein made in the liver and present in blood plasma. It converts into fibrin, another protein, during blood clotting.

Flask—container often having a narrow opening, fitted with a cover.

Fraternity—often a men's student organization formed for social purposes and usually bearing a name beginning with Greek letters.

Influenza—commonly known as the flu; a contagious disease that affects the respiratory system.

Intercollegiate—activities or competitions between colleges.

Jim Crow—an expression referring to any law or practice used to segregate black people.

Pathology—the nature of diseases and the changes in the body produced by diseases.

Plasma—the fluid of the blood, yellowish in color.

Post-operative—what happens after surgery.

Pre-operative—preparations made before surgery is performed.

Segregated—restricted or separated by group or race.

Sterilizing—making something clean by using extreme heat to kill microscopic organisms.

Surgeon—a medical specialist who performs operations.

Thesis—a long written work based on original research.

Transfusions—the transfer of blood into a vein of a person or animal.

Tuberculosis—a contagious disease that affects the lungs.

FOR FURTHER READING

Bittker, Anne S. "Charles Richard Drew, M.D." *Negro History Bulletin* 26 (June 1950): 144–50.

Cobb, W. Montague. "Charles Richard Drew, M.D., 1904–1950." *Negro History Bulletin* 42 (July 1950): 238–46.

Croman, Dorothy Young. *Sprinter in Life: Charles Richard Drew.* Nashville, Tenn.: Winston-Derek Publishers, Inc., 1988.

Drew, Charles. "The Role of Soviet Investigators in the Development of the Blood Bank." *American Review of Soviet Medicine* 1 (April 1944): 360–69.

Drew, Lenore Robbins. "Unforgettable Charlie Drew." *Reader's Digest,* March 1978.

Mahone-Lonesome, Robyn. *Charles Drew, Physician.* New York: Chelsea House Publishers, 1990.

Richardson, Ben, and William A. Fahey. *Great Black Americans.* New York: Thomas Crowell Co., 1976.

Wynes, Charles E. *Charles Richard Drew: The Man and the Myth.* Urbana, Ill.: University of Illinois Press, 1988.

INDEX